Ignite Your Inner Drive

Unleash the Power of Motivation to Transform Your Life

Vivian Pope

loss due to the information herein, either directly or indirectly. Respective authors own all copyrights not held by the publisher. The information herein is offered for informational purposes solely, and is universal as so. The presentation of the information is without contract or any type of guarantee assurance. The trademarks that are used are without any consent, and the publication of the trademark is without permission or backing by the trademark owner. All trademarks and brands within this book are for clarifying purposes only and are the owned by the owners themselves, not affiliated with this document.

Table of Contents

Chapter 1

Understanding Motivation

The Science Behind Motivation

Motivation is a complex and multifaceted phenomenon that has intrigued scientists, psychologists, and philosophers for centuries. At its core, motivation is the driving force that compels individuals to take action, pursue goals, and achieve desired outcomes. Understanding the science behind motivation involves delving into the intricate interplay of biological, psychological, and social factors that influence human behavior.

Biologically, motivation is deeply rooted in the brain's reward system. The neurotransmitter dopamine plays a crucial role in regulating motivation by signaling pleasure and reward. When an individual engages in an activity that is perceived as rewarding, dopamine is released, reinforcing the behavior and encouraging its repetition. This process is fundamental to understanding why certain activities are more motivating than others. For instance, the anticipation of a reward can trigger a surge of dopamine, creating a sense of excitement and eagerness to pursue the task at hand.

Psychologically, motivation is influenced by a variety of factors, including needs, desires, and goals. Abraham Maslow's hierarchy of needs provides a framework for understanding how different levels of needs, from basic physiological requirements to higher-order self-actualization, drive motivation. According to Maslow, individuals are motivated to fulfill their basic needs before pursuing higher-level aspirations. This theory highlights the importance of addressing fundamental needs to unlock higher levels of motivation.

Another psychological theory that sheds light on motivation is the Self-Determination Theory (SDT), developed by Edward Deci and Richard Ryan. SDT posits that motivation is driven by three innate psychological needs: autonomy, competence, and relatedness. Autonomy refers to the need for individuals to feel in control of their actions and decisions. Competence involves the desire to master tasks and achieve goals, while relatedness pertains to the need for social connection and belonging. When these needs are satisfied, individuals experience intrinsic motivation, which is characterized by a genuine interest and enjoyment in the activity itself, rather than external rewards or pressures.

The distinction between intrinsic and extrinsic motivation is a key concept in understanding the science of motivation. Intrinsic motivation arises from within the individual and is driven by personal satisfaction and interest in the task. In contrast, extrinsic motivation is influenced by external factors such as rewards, recognition, or avoidance of punishment. While both types of motivation can be effective in driving behavior, research suggests that intrinsic motivation is more sustainable and leads to greater long-term satisfaction and performance.

Emotions also play a significant role in motivation. Positive emotions, such as joy, excitement, and enthusiasm, can enhance motivation by creating a sense of energy and engagement. Conversely, negative emotions, such as fear, anxiety, and frustration, can either hinder or spur motivation, depending on how they are managed. For example, fear of failure may demotivate some individuals, while others may use it as a catalyst to work harder and overcome challenges.

Social factors, including cultural norms, social expectations, and interpersonal relationships, also influence motivation. The social environment can either support or undermine an individual's motivation. For instance, a supportive and encouraging social network can boost motivation by providing validation and encouragement. On the other hand, a critical or unsupportive environment can diminish motivation by fostering self-doubt and discouragement.

Motivation is not a static trait but rather a dynamic process that can fluctuate over time. Various factors, such as changes in personal circumstances, shifts in priorities, and external influences, can impact an individual's level of motivation. Understanding the science behind motivation involves recognizing these fluctuations and developing strategies to sustain motivation over the long term.

One effective strategy for enhancing motivation is goal setting. Setting clear, specific, and achievable goals provides individuals with a sense of direction and purpose. Goals serve as a roadmap, guiding individuals toward desired outcomes and providing a benchmark for measuring progress. The process of setting and achieving goals can be highly motivating, as it creates a sense of accomplishment and reinforces the belief in one's abilities.

Another important aspect of motivation is self-regulation, which involves the ability to manage one's thoughts, emotions, and behaviors in pursuit of goals. Self-regulation requires individuals to monitor their progress, adjust their strategies, and maintain focus and discipline. Developing self-regulation skills can enhance motivation by enabling individuals to overcome obstacles and persist in the face of challenges.

The science of motivation also highlights the importance of feedback in sustaining motivation.

Feedback provides individuals with valuable information about their performance and progress, allowing them to make necessary adjustments and improvements. Constructive feedback can boost motivation by reinforcing positive behaviors and encouraging further effort. However, feedback that is overly critical or negative can undermine motivation by fostering self-doubt and discouragement.

In addition to these strategies, cultivating a growth mindset can significantly impact motivation. A growth mindset, as proposed by psychologist Carol Dweck, is the belief that abilities and intelligence can be developed through effort and learning. Individuals with a growth mindset view challenges as opportunities for growth and are more likely to persist in the face of setbacks. This mindset fosters resilience and a willingness to embrace new experiences, ultimately enhancing motivation.

Intrinsic vs. Extrinsic Motivation

Motivation is a powerful force that propels individuals toward their goals and aspirations. It can be broadly categorized into two types: intrinsic and extrinsic motivation. Understanding the distinction between these two forms of motivation is crucial for harnessing their potential and achieving personal growth.

Intrinsic motivation originates from within an individual. It is driven by personal interest, enjoyment, and a sense of fulfillment derived from the activity itself. When someone is intrinsically motivated, they engage in an activity because it is inherently rewarding, not because of any external incentives or pressures. This type of motivation is often associated with a deep sense of satisfaction and a genuine passion for the task at hand. For example, a musician who plays an instrument for the sheer joy of creating music, or a writer who crafts stories out of a love for storytelling, are both examples of intrinsic motivation in action.

The benefits of intrinsic motivation are manifold. It fosters creativity, as individuals are more likely to explore new ideas and take risks when they are driven by genuine interest. It also enhances persistence, as people are more likely to persevere through challenges when they are motivated by internal satisfaction rather than external rewards. Furthermore, intrinsic motivation is linked to higher levels of well-being and happiness, as individuals experience a sense of autonomy and self-determination in their pursuits.

On the other hand, extrinsic motivation is driven by external factors such as rewards, recognition, or the avoidance of negative consequences. When someone is extrinsically motivated, they engage in an activity to achieve a specific outcome or to gain approval from others. This type of motivation is often associated with tangible rewards, such as money, grades, or accolades. For instance, an employee who works overtime to earn a bonus, or a student who studies diligently to receive high grades, are both examples of extrinsic motivation at play.

While extrinsic motivation can be effective in driving behavior, it has its limitations. It may lead to a focus on short-term gains rather than long-term growth, as individuals may prioritize immediate rewards over deeper learning or personal development. Additionally, extrinsic motivation can diminish intrinsic motivation if individuals become overly reliant on external incentives. This phenomenon, known as the overjustification effect, occurs when the introduction of external rewards undermines an individual's internal interest in an activity.

Despite these limitations, extrinsic motivation can be a valuable tool when used appropriately. It can provide the initial push needed to start a task or to overcome inertia. For example, offering a reward for completing a challenging project can motivate individuals to take the first step and build momentum. Extrinsic motivation can also be effective in situations where tasks are mundane or uninteresting, as it provides an external reason to engage in the activity.

The key to leveraging both intrinsic and extrinsic motivation lies in finding the right balance. By aligning external incentives with internal interests, individuals can create a synergistic effect that enhances motivation and performance. For example, a teacher who incorporates students' interests into the curriculum while also providing positive feedback and recognition can foster both intrinsic and extrinsic motivation in the classroom.

To cultivate intrinsic motivation, individuals can focus on activities that align with their passions and values. By identifying what truly excites and fulfills them, they can engage in pursuits that bring joy and satisfaction. Setting meaningful goals that resonate with personal values can also enhance intrinsic motivation, as individuals are more likely to be motivated by goals that reflect their true selves.

On the other hand, extrinsic motivation can be harnessed by setting clear and achievable rewards for specific tasks. By establishing a system of incentives that aligns with personal goals, individuals can create a motivating environment that encourages progress and achievement. It is important, however, to ensure that external rewards do not overshadow the intrinsic value of the activity, as this can lead to a decrease in internal motivation.

In the workplace, managers can foster motivation by recognizing and rewarding employees' efforts while also providing opportunities for personal growth and development. By creating a supportive and empowering environment, organizations can enhance both intrinsic and extrinsic motivation, leading to increased productivity and job satisfaction.

In educational settings, teachers can promote motivation by designing engaging and relevant learning experiences that tap into students' interests and passions. By providing constructive feedback and celebrating achievements, educators can encourage both intrinsic and extrinsic motivation, leading to improved learning outcomes and student engagement.

The Role of Emotions in Motivation

Emotions are an integral part of the human experience, influencing our thoughts, behaviors, and decisions. They play a significant role in shaping motivation, acting as both catalysts and barriers to action. Understanding the interplay between emotions and motivation can provide valuable insights into how individuals can harness their emotional states to achieve their goals and aspirations.

Emotions can be powerful motivators, driving individuals to pursue their desires and overcome obstacles. Positive emotions, such as joy, excitement, and satisfaction, can enhance motivation by creating a sense of enthusiasm and energy. When individuals experience positive emotions, they are more likely to engage in activities with vigor and persistence. For example, the exhilaration of achieving a personal milestone can propel someone to set even higher goals and strive for further success. Similarly, the anticipation of a rewarding experience can motivate individuals to take the necessary steps to make it a reality.

Conversely, negative emotions, such as fear, anger, and frustration, can also influence motivation, albeit in different ways. While these emotions can sometimes hinder motivation by creating feelings of doubt or discouragement, they can also serve as powerful motivators when channeled effectively. Fear, for instance, can prompt individuals to take precautionary measures or to prepare more thoroughly for a challenge. Anger can fuel determination and drive individuals to take action against perceived injustices or obstacles. The key lies in recognizing and managing these emotions to prevent them from becoming overwhelming or paralyzing.

Emotional intelligence, the ability to recognize, understand, and manage one's emotions, plays a crucial role in harnessing the motivational power of emotions. Individuals with high emotional intelligence are better equipped to navigate their emotional landscapes, using their emotions to inform and guide their actions. By developing emotional intelligence, individuals can learn to identify the emotions that drive their motivation and leverage them to achieve their goals.

One way to enhance emotional intelligence is through self-awareness, which involves recognizing and understanding one's emotional states. By becoming more attuned to their emotions, individuals can gain insights into what motivates them and how their emotions influence their behavior. This self-awareness can help individuals identify patterns in their emotional responses and develop strategies to manage them effectively.

Another important aspect of emotional intelligence is self-regulation, the ability to manage and control one's emotions. By practicing self-regulation, individuals can learn to channel their emotions in constructive ways, using them to fuel motivation rather than allowing them to become obstacles. Techniques such as mindfulness, deep breathing, and cognitive reframing can help individuals regulate their emotions and maintain focus on their goals.

Empathy, the ability to understand and share the feelings of others, is also a key component of emotional intelligence. By cultivating empathy, individuals can enhance their motivation by connecting with the emotions and experiences of others. This connection can create a sense of purpose and drive individuals to take action in support of others or to contribute to a greater cause. For example, witnessing the struggles of others can inspire individuals to advocate for change or to offer support and assistance.

Social skills, the ability to interact effectively with others, are another important aspect of emotional intelligence. By developing strong social skills, individuals can build supportive relationships that enhance motivation. Positive social interactions can create a sense of belonging and encouragement, motivating individuals to pursue their goals with confidence. Additionally, social support can provide valuable resources and feedback, helping individuals stay motivated and on track.

The relationship between emotions and motivation is not static; it is dynamic and influenced by various factors, including individual differences, situational contexts, and cultural norms. Understanding these influences can help individuals tailor their motivational strategies to their unique circumstances. For example, cultural norms may shape the way emotions are expressed and perceived, influencing how individuals experience and respond to motivation. By being mindful of these cultural influences, individuals can develop culturally sensitive approaches to motivation that resonate with their values and beliefs.

Situational contexts, such as the environment or the presence of stressors, can also impact the relationship between emotions and motivation. In high-pressure situations, individuals may experience heightened emotions that can either enhance or hinder motivation. By developing coping strategies to manage stress and maintain emotional balance, individuals can navigate challenging situations with resilience and determination.

Individual differences, such as personality traits and temperament, can also play a role in shaping the relationship between emotions and motivation. Some individuals may be naturally more optimistic and resilient, while others may be more prone to anxiety or self-doubt. By understanding their unique emotional profiles, individuals can develop personalized strategies to harness their emotions and enhance motivation.

Common Myths About Motivation

Motivation is a complex and multifaceted concept that has intrigued scholars, psychologists, and everyday individuals alike. Despite its importance in driving human behavior, motivation is often misunderstood, leading to the proliferation of myths that can hinder personal growth and achievement. By debunking these common myths, individuals can gain a clearer understanding of motivation and develop more effective strategies for achieving their goals.

One prevalent myth is the belief that motivation is a fixed trait, something that individuals either possess or lack. This misconception suggests that motivation is an inherent quality, akin to eye color or height, and that those who are not naturally motivated are doomed to struggle. In reality, motivation is not a static trait but a dynamic state that can be cultivated and nurtured. It is influenced by a variety of factors, including personal interests, values, and external circumstances. By recognizing that motivation can be developed, individuals can take proactive steps to enhance their motivation through goal setting, self-reflection, and the cultivation of positive habits.

Another common myth is the idea that motivation is solely driven by external rewards, such as money, recognition, or praise. While external incentives can certainly play a role in motivating behavior, they are not the only, or even the most effective, source of motivation. Intrinsic motivation, which arises from internal factors such as personal satisfaction, curiosity, and a sense of purpose, is often more powerful and sustainable than extrinsic motivation. Individuals who are intrinsically motivated are more likely to engage in activities with enthusiasm and persistence, even in the absence of external rewards. By identifying and nurturing their intrinsic motivations, individuals can cultivate a deeper and more enduring sense of motivation.

The notion that motivation is a constant, unwavering force is another myth that can lead to frustration and disappointment. Many people believe that once they find motivation, it will remain steady and unchanging, propelling them effortlessly toward their goals. However, motivation is inherently variable and can fluctuate based on a range of factors, including mood, energy levels, and external circumstances. It is natural for motivation to ebb and flow, and individuals should not be discouraged by temporary dips in motivation. Instead, they can develop strategies to reignite their motivation during challenging times, such as revisiting their goals, seeking inspiration from others, or taking small, manageable steps toward progress.

A related myth is the belief that motivation is always accompanied by a sense of excitement and enthusiasm. While motivation can certainly be energizing, it is not always characterized by intense emotions or a constant state of exhilaration. In fact, motivation can sometimes manifest as a quiet determination or a steady commitment to a goal. Individuals may not always feel a surge of excitement when pursuing their goals, but this does not mean they lack motivation. By recognizing that motivation can take different forms, individuals can maintain their focus and persistence even when their emotional state is more subdued.

The myth that motivation is solely an individual endeavor is another misconception that can limit personal growth. While motivation is indeed a personal experience, it is also influenced by social and environmental factors. Supportive relationships, positive social interactions, and a conducive environment can all enhance motivation by providing encouragement, feedback, and resources. Conversely, negative social influences or an unsupportive environment can undermine motivation and hinder progress. By seeking out supportive networks and creating an environment that fosters motivation, individuals can enhance their ability to achieve their goals.

The belief that motivation is synonymous with willpower is another myth that can lead to misunderstandings about the nature of motivation. While willpower, or the ability to exert self-control and resist temptations, is an important aspect of motivation, it is not the only factor at play. Motivation is a multifaceted construct that encompasses a range of psychological processes, including goal setting, self-efficacy, and emotional regulation. By understanding the various components of motivation, individuals can develop a more comprehensive approach to enhancing their motivation and achieving their goals.

The myth that motivation is a one-size-fits-all solution is another misconception that can hinder personal growth. Different individuals are motivated by different factors, and what works for one person may not work for another. Some individuals may be motivated by competition and achievement, while others may be driven by collaboration and connection. By recognizing and embracing their unique motivational profiles, individuals can tailor their strategies to align with their personal preferences and values.

The idea that motivation is only necessary for achieving grand, ambitious goals is another myth that can limit personal growth. While motivation is certainly important for pursuing significant achievements, it is also essential for everyday tasks and activities. Motivation can drive individuals to complete mundane chores, maintain healthy habits, and engage in meaningful relationships. By recognizing the role of motivation in all aspects of life, individuals can cultivate a sense of purpose and fulfillment in both their everyday routines and their long-term aspirations.

The myth that motivation is an all-or-nothing phenomenon is another misconception that can lead to frustration and self-doubt. Many people believe that they must be fully motivated at all times to achieve their goals, and that any lapse in motivation is a sign of failure. In reality, motivation is a spectrum, and individuals can experience varying degrees of motivation at different times. It is normal to have moments of doubt or hesitation, and these moments do not negate the overall motivation to achieve a goal. By acknowledging and accepting the natural fluctuations in motivation, individuals can maintain their focus and persistence even in the face of challenges.

The belief that motivation is solely a mental construct is another myth that can limit personal growth. While motivation is indeed a psychological phenomenon, it is also influenced by physical factors such as energy levels, nutrition, and sleep. Physical well-being can have a significant impact on motivation, and individuals who neglect their physical health may find it difficult to maintain motivation. By prioritizing physical well-being and adopting healthy lifestyle habits, individuals can enhance their motivation and overall sense of well-being.

How Motivation Influences Behavior

Motivation serves as the invisible force that propels individuals toward action, shaping behavior in profound and often subtle ways. It is the catalyst that transforms intention into action, bridging the gap between desire and achievement. Understanding how motivation influences behavior requires an exploration of the intricate interplay between internal drives, external stimuli, and the cognitive processes that mediate this relationship.

At its core, motivation is the psychological process that initiates, guides, and sustains goal-directed behavior. It is the reason behind the choices individuals make, the persistence they exhibit, and the intensity with which they pursue their goals. Motivation can be driven by a variety of factors, including biological needs, personal values, social influences, and environmental conditions. These factors interact to create a complex motivational landscape that influences behavior in diverse and dynamic ways.

One of the primary ways motivation influences behavior is through the setting and pursuit of goals. Goals provide direction and purpose, serving as the targets toward which motivated behavior is directed. When individuals set clear and specific goals, they are more likely to engage in behaviors that align with those goals. The process of goal setting involves identifying desired outcomes, establishing criteria for success, and developing action plans to achieve those outcomes. Motivation plays a crucial role in this process by providing the energy and focus needed to pursue goals with determination and persistence.

The influence of motivation on behavior is also evident in the way individuals allocate their attention and resources. Motivated individuals are more likely to prioritize tasks and activities that are relevant to their goals, directing their attention and effort toward actions that will bring them closer to achieving their desired outcomes. This selective attention allows individuals to filter out distractions and maintain focus on their objectives, enhancing their ability to make progress and overcome obstacles.

Motivation also affects behavior through its impact on decision-making processes. When individuals are motivated, they are more likely to engage in thoughtful and deliberate decision-making, weighing the potential costs and benefits of different courses of action. Motivation can enhance cognitive processes such as problem-solving, planning, and critical thinking, enabling individuals to make informed choices that align with their goals. Conversely, a lack of motivation can lead to impulsive or hasty decisions, as individuals may be less inclined to consider the long-term consequences of their actions.

The relationship between motivation and behavior is further influenced by the concept of self-efficacy, or the belief in one's ability to succeed in specific situations. Self-efficacy is a key determinant of motivation, as individuals who believe in their capabilities are more likely to set challenging goals, persist in the face of adversity, and exhibit resilience when confronted with setbacks. Motivation and self-efficacy are mutually reinforcing, with motivation enhancing self-efficacy by providing the drive to develop skills and competencies, and self-efficacy bolstering motivation by fostering confidence and a sense of agency.

Motivation also plays a critical role in regulating emotions and managing stress, both of which can significantly impact behavior. Motivated individuals are more likely to employ adaptive coping strategies, such as problem-solving and seeking social support, to manage stress and maintain emotional well-being. By regulating emotions and reducing stress, motivation enables individuals to maintain focus and persistence, even in challenging circumstances. This emotional regulation is essential for sustaining motivation over the long term and achieving desired outcomes.

The influence of motivation on behavior is not limited to individual actions but extends to social interactions and relationships. Motivated individuals are more likely to engage in prosocial behaviors, such as cooperation, collaboration, and altruism, which can enhance social bonds and foster a sense of community. Motivation can also drive individuals to seek out social support and feedback, which can provide valuable resources and encouragement for achieving their goals. By influencing social behavior, motivation contributes to the development of supportive networks and positive social environments that can further enhance motivation and facilitate goal attainment.

The dynamic nature of motivation means that its influence on behavior can change over time, depending on a variety of factors. Motivation can be influenced by changes in personal circumstances, such as shifts in priorities, values, or life events, as well as by external factors, such as changes in the social or environmental context. This variability highlights the importance of flexibility and adaptability in maintaining motivation and achieving goals. Individuals who are able to adjust their motivational strategies in response to changing circumstances are more likely to sustain motivation and achieve long-term success.

Understanding the ways in which motivation influences behavior can provide valuable insights for individuals seeking to enhance their motivation and achieve their goals. By recognizing the factors that drive motivation and the processes through which it influences behavior, individuals can develop more effective strategies for goal setting, decision-making, and emotional regulation. This understanding can also inform the development of interventions and programs designed to enhance motivation and support behavior change in a variety of contexts, from education and health to work and personal development.

Chapter 2

Identifying Your Personal Motivators

Discovering Your Core Values

Understanding one's core values is akin to uncovering the compass that guides life's journey. These values are the fundamental beliefs and principles that shape decisions, influence behavior, and define what is truly important. They serve as the foundation upon which individuals build their lives, providing clarity and direction in a world often filled with uncertainty and complexity.

The process of discovering core values begins with introspection and self-reflection. It requires a willingness to delve deep into one's thoughts, emotions, and experiences to identify the beliefs that resonate most profoundly. This journey of self-discovery is not always straightforward, as it involves peeling back layers of social conditioning, expectations, and external influences to reveal the authentic self. It is a process that demands honesty, vulnerability, and courage.

One effective method for uncovering core values is to reflect on past experiences and identify moments of profound satisfaction or fulfillment. These moments often provide clues to the values that are most important. For instance, an individual who feels a deep sense of fulfillment when helping others may value compassion and altruism. Similarly, someone who derives satisfaction from creative expression may prioritize creativity and innovation. By examining these experiences, individuals can begin to identify patterns and themes that point to their core values.

Another approach to discovering core values is to consider the qualities and characteristics admired in others. These qualities often reflect the values that individuals aspire to embody in their own lives. By identifying role models and examining the traits that make them admirable, individuals can gain insight into the values they hold dear. This process not only helps clarify personal values but also provides inspiration and motivation to live in alignment with those values.

It is also important to consider the values that evoke strong emotional responses, whether positive or negative. Values that elicit strong emotions are often deeply ingrained and can serve as powerful motivators for behavior. For example, an individual who feels a strong sense of injustice in the face of inequality may value fairness and equity. By paying attention to these emotional responses, individuals can gain a deeper understanding of the values that drive their actions and decisions.

Once core values have been identified, it is essential to prioritize them and consider how they align with current life circumstances. This involves evaluating whether one's actions, relationships, and goals are consistent with their values. When there is alignment between values and behavior, individuals are more likely to experience a sense of authenticity and fulfillment. Conversely, when there is a disconnect between values and behavior, individuals may experience inner conflict and dissatisfaction.

Living in alignment with core values requires intentionality and commitment. It involves making conscious choices that reflect one's values, even in the face of challenges or external pressures. This may mean setting boundaries, making difficult decisions, or pursuing goals that align with one's values, even when they are not the easiest or most convenient options. By consistently choosing to live in accordance with their values, individuals can cultivate a sense of integrity and authenticity that enhances their overall well-being.

The discovery of core values is not a one-time event but an ongoing process that evolves over time. As individuals grow and change, their values may also shift, reflecting new insights, experiences, and priorities. It is important to regularly revisit and reassess core values to ensure they remain relevant and meaningful. This process of continual reflection and adaptation allows individuals to stay true to themselves and navigate life's challenges with clarity and purpose.

In addition to personal reflection, engaging in open and honest conversations with trusted friends, family members, or mentors can provide valuable perspectives and insights into one's core values. These conversations can help individuals gain a deeper understanding of their values and how they manifest in their lives. By seeking feedback and engaging in dialogue, individuals can refine their understanding of their values and explore new ways to live in alignment with them.

Ultimately, discovering core values is a deeply personal and transformative journey that empowers individuals to live with intention and purpose. By uncovering and embracing their values, individuals can create a life that is authentic, meaningful, and fulfilling. This journey of self-discovery not only enhances personal well-being but also contributes to the development of a more compassionate and connected world, as individuals who live in alignment with their values are more likely to engage in behaviors that promote positive social change.

Setting Meaningful Goals

Setting meaningful goals is a transformative process that can significantly impact one's life trajectory. Goals serve as the roadmap guiding individuals toward their desired future, providing a sense of purpose and direction. They are not merely aspirations but concrete steps that bridge the gap between where one is and where one wants to be. The art of goal-setting involves more than just identifying what one wants to achieve; it requires a thoughtful and strategic approach to ensure that goals are both meaningful and attainable.

The first step in setting meaningful goals is to engage in self-reflection and introspection. This involves examining one's values, passions, and long-term vision for life. Understanding what truly matters is crucial in identifying goals that resonate on a deeper level. For instance, someone who values personal growth may set goals related to learning new skills or pursuing educational opportunities. By aligning goals with core values, individuals can ensure that their pursuits are not only meaningful but also fulfilling.

Once there is clarity on what is important, it is essential to articulate goals in a clear and specific manner. Vague or ambiguous goals can lead to confusion and lack of motivation. Instead, goals should be defined with precision, outlining exactly what is to be achieved and by when. For example, rather than setting a goal to "get fit," one might specify the goal as "run a 5k marathon in six months." This specificity provides a clear target to work toward and makes it easier to track progress.

In addition to being specific, goals should be challenging yet realistic. Setting overly ambitious goals can lead to frustration and discouragement, while setting goals that are too easy may not provide the necessary motivation to strive for improvement. It is important to strike a balance by setting goals that push one's limits while remaining achievable. This balance fosters a sense of accomplishment and encourages continued effort and perseverance.

Breaking down larger goals into smaller, manageable tasks is another effective strategy in goal-setting. This approach not only makes the process less overwhelming but also provides a sense of progress and momentum. Each small task completed brings one closer to the ultimate goal, reinforcing motivation and commitment. For instance, if the goal is to write a book, breaking it down into tasks such as outlining chapters, writing a certain number of words each day, and editing drafts can make the process more manageable and less daunting.

Accountability plays a crucial role in the pursuit of meaningful goals. Sharing goals with trusted friends, family members, or mentors can provide support and encouragement, as well as hold individuals accountable for their progress. Regular check-ins and updates can help maintain focus and motivation, while also providing an opportunity to celebrate achievements and milestones along the way. Additionally, accountability partners can offer valuable feedback and insights, helping to refine and adjust goals as needed.

Flexibility is another important aspect of setting meaningful goals. Life is unpredictable, and circumstances can change, requiring individuals to adapt and adjust their goals accordingly. Being open to reevaluating and modifying goals in response to new information or changing priorities is essential for maintaining relevance and motivation. This flexibility allows individuals to remain resilient and adaptable, ensuring that their goals continue to align with their evolving vision and values.

Visualization and positive affirmation techniques can also enhance the goal-setting process. By vividly imagining the successful achievement of a goal, individuals can create a mental image that reinforces motivation and commitment. Positive affirmations, on the other hand, can help cultivate a mindset of confidence and self-belief, counteracting any doubts or fears that may arise. These techniques can serve as powerful tools in maintaining focus and determination throughout the journey.

Tracking progress and celebrating achievements are integral components of setting meaningful goals. Regularly assessing progress allows individuals to identify areas of improvement and make necessary adjustments. Celebrating achievements, no matter how small, reinforces motivation and provides a sense of accomplishment. This positive reinforcement encourages continued effort and perseverance, ultimately leading to the successful attainment of goals.

The journey of setting and achieving meaningful goals is a dynamic and evolving process. It requires a commitment to self-discovery, strategic planning, and continuous adaptation. By setting goals that align with one's values and vision, individuals can create a life that is purposeful and fulfilling. This process not only enhances personal growth and development but also contributes to a greater sense of satisfaction and well-being.

In the pursuit of meaningful goals, it is important to remain patient and persistent. Progress may not always be linear, and setbacks are a natural part of the journey. However, by maintaining a positive attitude and staying committed to the process, individuals can overcome obstacles and achieve their desired outcomes. The journey itself is as valuable as the destination, offering opportunities for learning, growth, and self-discovery.

The Impact of Passion on Motivation

Passion is a powerful force that can ignite the flames of motivation, driving individuals to pursue their goals with unwavering determination. It is the emotional fuel that propels people forward, even in the face of challenges and setbacks. Understanding the impact of passion on motivation is essential for anyone seeking to achieve their aspirations and live a fulfilling life.

At its core, passion is an intense enthusiasm or fervor for something that holds personal significance. It is the deep-seated interest that captivates the mind and heart, inspiring individuals to invest time and energy into their pursuits. When passion is present, motivation becomes a natural byproduct, as individuals are driven by an intrinsic desire to engage in activities that bring them joy and satisfaction.

One of the most significant ways passion influences motivation is by creating a sense of purpose. When individuals are passionate about a particular endeavor, they are more likely to view it as meaningful and worthwhile. This sense of purpose provides a clear direction and focus, guiding individuals toward their goals with a sense of clarity and intention. It transforms mundane tasks into opportunities for growth and learning, making the journey as rewarding as the destination.

Passion also enhances motivation by fostering resilience and perseverance. In the pursuit of any goal, obstacles and setbacks are inevitable. However, when individuals are passionate about what they are doing, they are more likely to view challenges as opportunities for growth rather than insurmountable barriers. Passionate individuals possess a tenacity that enables them to push through difficulties, maintaining their motivation even when the going gets tough. This resilience is a key factor in achieving long-term success and fulfillment.

Moreover, passion can lead to a state of flow, a psychological phenomenon characterized by complete immersion and focus in an activity. When individuals are in a state of flow, they experience heightened creativity, productivity, and satisfaction. Passion acts as a catalyst for entering this state, as it allows individuals to lose themselves in their work, fully engaged and absorbed in the task at hand. This deep level of engagement not only enhances motivation but also leads to higher levels of performance and achievement.

The impact of passion on motivation is also evident in the way it influences goal-setting. Passionate individuals are more likely to set ambitious and challenging goals, as they are driven by a desire to excel and make a meaningful impact. These goals are often aligned with their values and interests, making them more personally significant and motivating. The pursuit of such goals becomes a source of inspiration and excitement, fueling motivation and commitment.

Furthermore, passion can have a contagious effect, inspiring and motivating others. When individuals are passionate about their work or interests, their enthusiasm is often infectious, influencing those around them. This ripple effect can create a supportive and motivating environment, where individuals are encouraged to pursue their passions and strive for excellence. The collective energy and motivation generated by a group of passionate individuals can lead to remarkable achievements and innovations.

However, it is important to recognize that passion alone is not enough to sustain motivation. While passion provides the initial spark, it must be complemented by discipline, planning, and effort to achieve lasting success. Passionate individuals must be willing to put in the hard work and dedication required to turn their dreams into reality. This involves setting clear goals, developing a strategic plan, and consistently taking action toward their objectives.

Additionally, it is essential to maintain a balance between passion and practicality. While passion can drive motivation, it is important to ensure that pursuits are realistic and sustainable. Overcommitting or neglecting other important aspects of life in the pursuit of passion can lead to burnout and diminished motivation. Striking a balance between passion and other responsibilities is crucial for maintaining long-term motivation and well-being.

In some cases, individuals may struggle to identify their passions or feel uncertain about what truly motivates them. In such instances, it can be helpful to explore different interests and activities, experimenting with new experiences to discover what resonates on a deeper level. This process of exploration can lead to the discovery of new passions and sources of motivation, opening up new possibilities and opportunities for growth.

Recognizing and Overcoming Limiting Beliefs

Limiting beliefs are the invisible chains that bind individuals, holding them back from reaching their full potential. These beliefs, often deeply ingrained and subconscious, shape perceptions of what is possible and influence decisions and actions.

Recognizing and overcoming these mental barriers is crucial for personal growth and success.

Limiting beliefs typically originate from past experiences, societal conditioning, or negative self-talk. They manifest as thoughts or assumptions that restrict possibilities, such as "I'm not good enough," "I don't deserve success," or "I'll never be able to do that." These beliefs can be insidious, subtly influencing behavior and creating self-imposed limitations that hinder progress.

The first step in overcoming limiting beliefs is to identify them. This requires introspection and self-awareness, as these beliefs often operate below the surface of conscious thought. Reflecting on areas of life where progress feels stalled or where fear and doubt are prevalent can provide clues to underlying limiting beliefs. Journaling, meditation, or speaking with a trusted friend or mentor can facilitate this process, helping to bring these beliefs to light.

Once identified, it is important to challenge the validity of these beliefs. Often, limiting beliefs are based on assumptions or interpretations rather than objective reality. Questioning the evidence supporting these beliefs and considering alternative perspectives can weaken their hold. For example, if the belief is "I'm not good enough," examining past achievements and strengths can provide evidence to the contrary, highlighting capabilities and potential.

Reframing limiting beliefs into empowering ones is a powerful strategy for overcoming them. This involves transforming negative statements into positive affirmations that reflect a more accurate and constructive view of oneself. For instance, "I can't succeed" can be reframed as "I have the skills and determination to succeed." Repeatedly affirming these positive beliefs can help rewire thought patterns, replacing limiting beliefs with empowering ones.

Visualization is another effective tool for overcoming limiting beliefs. By vividly imagining oneself achieving goals and experiencing success, individuals can create a mental blueprint for success. This process helps to build confidence and reinforce positive beliefs, making them more tangible and attainable. Visualization can be practiced regularly, serving as a reminder of one's potential and capabilities.

Taking action is essential in breaking free from the constraints of limiting beliefs. Small, incremental steps toward goals can build momentum and demonstrate that change is possible. Each success, no matter how minor, serves as evidence that limiting beliefs are not insurmountable barriers. Celebrating these achievements reinforces positive beliefs and encourages continued progress.

Surrounding oneself with supportive and positive influences can also aid in overcoming limiting beliefs. Engaging with individuals who inspire and uplift can provide encouragement and motivation, challenging negative self-perceptions. Mentors, coaches, or supportive peers can offer guidance and perspective, helping to dismantle limiting beliefs and foster a growth mindset.

It is important to recognize that overcoming limiting beliefs is an ongoing process. These beliefs may resurface at different stages of life or in response to new challenges. Maintaining self-awareness and regularly revisiting strategies for overcoming limiting beliefs can help to prevent them from regaining power. Continuous personal development and learning can further strengthen resilience and adaptability, equipping individuals to face new obstacles with confidence.

In some cases, professional support may be beneficial in addressing deeply rooted limiting beliefs. Therapists or counselors can provide specialized techniques and insights to help individuals work through complex emotional barriers. Cognitive-behavioral therapy, for example, is an evidence-based approach that can effectively address and reframe limiting beliefs, promoting healthier thought patterns and behaviors.

Aligning Motivation with Personal Purpose

Motivation is the driving force that propels individuals toward their goals, yet it often fluctuates, leaving many to wonder how to sustain it over time. The key to maintaining motivation lies in aligning it with one's personal purpose. When motivation is rooted in a deeper sense of purpose, it becomes more resilient and enduring, providing a steady source of energy and inspiration.

Personal purpose is the unique combination of values, passions, and aspirations that define an individual's sense of meaning and direction in life. It is the compass that guides decisions and actions, offering clarity and focus. Understanding one's personal purpose requires introspection and self-discovery, as it is deeply personal and varies from person to person. It is not uncommon for individuals to spend years exploring and refining their sense of purpose, as it evolves with life experiences and changing priorities.

To align motivation with personal purpose, it is essential to first articulate what truly matters. This involves identifying core values and passions, as well as long-term goals and aspirations. Reflecting on past experiences and moments of fulfillment can provide valuable insights into what brings joy and satisfaction. Journaling, meditation, or engaging in meaningful conversations with trusted friends or mentors can facilitate this process, helping to uncover the underlying motivations that drive behavior.

Once personal purpose is defined, it is important to connect it to daily activities and goals. This requires a conscious effort to ensure that actions and decisions are aligned with one's values and aspirations. Setting goals that resonate with personal purpose can enhance motivation, as they are perceived as meaningful and worthwhile. These goals should be specific, measurable, achievable, relevant, and time-bound (SMART), providing a clear roadmap for progress.

Breaking down larger goals into smaller, manageable tasks can make them more approachable and less overwhelming. Each completed task serves as a stepping stone toward the larger goal, reinforcing motivation and providing a sense of accomplishment. Celebrating these small victories can boost morale and maintain momentum, reminding individuals of the progress they are making toward their purpose.

It is also important to cultivate a positive mindset and attitude, as these can significantly impact motivation. Embracing a growth mindset, which views challenges as opportunities for learning and development, can foster resilience and perseverance. Practicing gratitude and focusing on positive aspects of life can enhance well-being and motivation, creating a more optimistic outlook.

Surrounding oneself with supportive and like-minded individuals can further strengthen motivation. Engaging with a community that shares similar values and goals can provide encouragement, accountability, and inspiration. Mentors, coaches, or peers can offer guidance and perspective, helping to navigate challenges and stay focused on personal purpose.

Maintaining motivation also requires self-care and balance. It is important to prioritize physical, mental, and emotional well-being, as these are foundational to sustained motivation. Regular exercise, a healthy diet, adequate sleep, and stress management techniques can enhance energy levels and overall well-being. Taking time for relaxation and leisure activities can prevent burnout and promote a sense of balance, allowing individuals to recharge and refocus.

Flexibility and adaptability are also crucial in aligning motivation with personal purpose. Life is dynamic, and circumstances can change unexpectedly, requiring individuals to adjust their goals and plans. Being open to change and willing to reassess and realign goals with personal purpose can ensure that motivation remains relevant and meaningful. This may involve letting go of goals that no longer serve one's purpose or exploring new opportunities that align with evolving values and aspirations.

Chapter 3

Building a Motivated Mindset

Cultivating a Growth Mindset

A growth mindset is a powerful tool that can transform the way individuals approach challenges, learning, and personal development. Coined by psychologist Carol Dweck, the concept of a growth mindset revolves around the belief that abilities and intelligence can be developed through dedication, effort, and perseverance. This contrasts with a fixed mindset, where individuals perceive their talents and intelligence as static traits that cannot be changed. Cultivating a growth mindset can lead to greater resilience, adaptability, and success in various aspects of life.

The journey toward developing a growth mindset begins with self-awareness. Recognizing one's current mindset is the first step in making a conscious shift. This involves reflecting on how one responds to challenges, setbacks, and feedback. Individuals with a fixed mindset may avoid challenges, give up easily, or feel threatened by the success of others. In contrast, those with a growth mindset embrace challenges, persist in the face of obstacles, and view the success of others as a source of inspiration.

To cultivate a growth mindset, it is essential to reframe the way one perceives challenges and failures. Instead of viewing them as indicators of inadequacy, they should be seen as opportunities for growth and learning. Embracing challenges with curiosity and a willingness to learn can foster resilience and a sense of accomplishment. This shift in perspective encourages individuals to step out of their comfort zones and take risks, knowing that mistakes and failures are valuable learning experiences.

Language plays a crucial role in shaping mindset. The words and phrases individuals use to describe themselves and their abilities can reinforce either a fixed or growth mindset. For example, saying "I'm not good at this" implies a fixed mindset, while saying "I'm not good at this yet" suggests a belief in the potential for improvement. By consciously choosing language that reflects a growth mindset, individuals can reinforce positive beliefs about their ability to learn and grow.

Feedback is another important aspect of cultivating a growth mindset. Constructive feedback provides valuable insights into areas for improvement and growth. Instead of viewing feedback as criticism, individuals with a growth mindset see it as an opportunity to learn and develop. Seeking feedback from others and being open to their perspectives can enhance self-awareness and facilitate personal growth. It is important to approach feedback with an open mind and a willingness to make changes, rather than becoming defensive or dismissive.

Setting goals that align with a growth mindset can further reinforce this perspective. These goals should focus on the process of learning and improvement, rather than solely on outcomes or achievements. For example, instead of setting a goal to achieve a specific grade or result, one might set a goal to develop a particular skill or to practice a new technique regularly. This approach emphasizes the importance of effort and persistence, rather than innate ability, and encourages continuous learning and development.

Cultivating a growth mindset also involves embracing the power of "yet." This simple word can transform the way individuals perceive their abilities and potential. When faced with a challenge or setback, adding "yet" to statements like "I can't do this" or "I don't understand this" can shift the focus from current limitations to future possibilities. This mindset fosters optimism and resilience, encouraging individuals to keep trying and to believe in their capacity for growth.

Surrounding oneself with a supportive and growth-oriented environment can further enhance the development of a growth mindset. Engaging with individuals who value learning, effort, and improvement can provide encouragement and inspiration. Mentors, coaches, or peers who embody a growth mindset can serve as role models, demonstrating the benefits of embracing challenges and persisting in the face of adversity. Collaborative learning and sharing experiences with others can also foster a sense of community and mutual support.

Practicing mindfulness and self-reflection can aid in cultivating a growth mindset. Mindfulness involves being present and aware of one's thoughts, emotions, and reactions without judgment. This practice can help individuals recognize when they are slipping into a fixed mindset and consciously choose to adopt a growth-oriented perspective. Regular self-reflection allows individuals to assess their progress, identify areas for improvement, and celebrate their achievements, reinforcing the belief in their ability to grow and develop.

It is important to recognize that cultivating a growth mindset is an ongoing process. It requires continuous effort and practice, as well as a willingness to challenge and change deeply ingrained beliefs and habits. Setbacks and challenges are inevitable, but they provide valuable opportunities for growth and learning. By maintaining a growth mindset, individuals can approach these experiences with resilience and determination, ultimately leading to greater success and fulfillment.

The Power of Positive Thinking

Positive thinking is a transformative force that can significantly impact one's life, influencing emotions, behaviors, and overall well-being. At its core, positive thinking involves maintaining an optimistic outlook, focusing on the good in any situation, and expecting favorable outcomes. This mindset can lead to improved mental health, increased resilience, and a greater sense of fulfillment. Understanding the power of positive thinking and how to harness it can be a game-changer for anyone seeking to enhance their quality of life.

The foundation of positive thinking lies in the ability to reframe negative thoughts and perceptions. Life is filled with challenges and setbacks, but how one chooses to interpret these events can make all the difference. Instead of dwelling on the negative aspects, positive thinkers look for the silver lining, finding opportunities for growth and learning in every situation. This shift in perspective not only reduces stress and anxiety but also fosters a sense of empowerment and control over one's life.

One of the key benefits of positive thinking is its impact on mental health. Studies have shown that individuals who consistently practice positive thinking experience lower levels of depression and anxiety. This is because positive thinking encourages the release of endorphins, the body's natural mood enhancers, which can lead to a more balanced emotional state. By focusing on positive thoughts and emotions, individuals can create a mental environment that supports mental well-being and resilience.

Positive thinking also plays a crucial role in physical health. Research has demonstrated that optimists tend to have stronger immune systems, lower blood pressure, and a reduced risk of chronic illnesses. This is partly due to the fact that positive thinkers are more likely to engage in healthy behaviors, such as regular exercise, balanced nutrition, and adequate sleep. Additionally, the stress-reducing effects of positive thinking can lead to a healthier cardiovascular system and improved overall health.

Cultivating positive thinking involves several practical strategies that can be easily incorporated into daily life. One effective approach is the practice of gratitude. By regularly acknowledging and appreciating the positive aspects of life, individuals can shift their focus away from negativity and foster a more optimistic outlook. Keeping a gratitude journal, where one records things they are thankful for each day, can be a powerful tool in reinforcing positive thinking.

Visualization is another technique that can enhance positive thinking. By vividly imagining desired outcomes and success, individuals can create a mental blueprint that guides their actions and decisions. This process not only boosts confidence and motivation but also helps to align thoughts and behaviors with one's goals. Visualization can be particularly effective when combined with affirmations, which are positive statements that reinforce self-belief and optimism.

Surrounding oneself with positive influences is also essential in nurturing a positive mindset. The people we interact with can significantly impact our thoughts and emotions. Engaging with individuals who exude positivity, encouragement, and support can inspire and uplift, creating an environment conducive to positive thinking. Conversely, distancing oneself from negative influences can prevent the spread of pessimism and doubt.

Mindfulness and meditation are powerful practices that can enhance positive thinking by promoting self-awareness and emotional regulation. Mindfulness involves being present in the moment, observing thoughts and feelings without judgment. This practice can help individuals recognize negative thought patterns and consciously choose to replace them with positive ones. Meditation, on the other hand, provides a space for relaxation and reflection, allowing individuals to cultivate a sense of inner peace and positivity.

The power of positive thinking extends beyond individual well-being, influencing relationships and social interactions. Optimistic individuals tend to have more fulfilling and harmonious relationships, as their positive outlook fosters empathy, understanding, and effective communication. By approaching interactions with kindness and positivity, individuals can build stronger connections and create a supportive social network.

In the realm of personal and professional success, positive thinking can be a driving force. Optimists are more likely to set ambitious goals, take calculated risks, and persevere in the face of challenges. This proactive approach often leads to greater achievements and satisfaction. Moreover, positive thinkers are more resilient, able to bounce back from setbacks and view failures as opportunities for growth and improvement.

While positive thinking is a powerful tool, it is important to acknowledge that it does not mean ignoring reality or avoiding difficult emotions. Instead, it involves a balanced approach that recognizes challenges while maintaining hope and optimism. By accepting and processing negative emotions, individuals can prevent them from becoming overwhelming and use them as catalysts for positive change.

Incorporating positive thinking into daily life requires commitment and practice. It involves consciously choosing to focus on the positive, even in challenging situations, and developing habits that reinforce an optimistic mindset. Over time, these practices can become second nature, leading to a more positive and fulfilling life.

Developing Resilience and Grit

Resilience and grit are two essential qualities that enable individuals to navigate life's challenges with strength and determination. These attributes are not innate; they can be cultivated and developed over time through intentional practice and mindset shifts. Understanding the significance of resilience and grit, and learning how to foster them, can empower individuals to overcome obstacles and achieve their goals.

Resilience is the ability to bounce back from adversity, setbacks, and failures. It involves maintaining a positive outlook and adapting to changing circumstances, even in the face of difficulty. Resilient individuals possess a sense of inner strength that allows them to persevere through tough times and emerge stronger on the other side. This quality is crucial in today's fast-paced and unpredictable world, where change is constant and challenges are inevitable.

Grit, on the other hand, is the passion and perseverance to pursue long-term goals. It involves a steadfast commitment to one's objectives, even when progress is slow or obstacles arise. Gritty individuals are characterized by their unwavering determination and willingness to put in the effort required to achieve their aspirations. This quality is often the differentiator between those who succeed and those who give up when faced with difficulties.

Developing resilience and grit begins with cultivating a growth mindset. This mindset, popularized by psychologist Carol Dweck, is the belief that abilities and intelligence can be developed through dedication and hard work. Individuals with a growth mindset view challenges as opportunities for growth and learning, rather than as threats to their self-worth. By embracing this perspective, individuals can build resilience and grit by seeing setbacks as stepping stones to success.

One practical way to develop resilience is by practicing self-compassion. This involves treating oneself with kindness and understanding, especially during times of failure or difficulty. Self-compassion allows individuals to acknowledge their imperfections without judgment, fostering a sense of acceptance and self-worth. By being gentle with themselves, individuals can build the emotional resilience needed to navigate life's ups and downs.

Another key aspect of resilience is the ability to regulate emotions. Emotional regulation involves recognizing and managing one's emotions in a healthy and constructive manner. This skill can be developed through mindfulness practices, such as meditation and deep breathing exercises, which promote self-awareness and emotional control. By learning to manage emotions effectively, individuals can respond to challenges with clarity and composure, rather than being overwhelmed by stress or anxiety.

Building grit requires setting clear and meaningful goals. Having a sense of purpose and direction provides the motivation needed to persevere through challenges. When setting goals, it is important to ensure they are specific, measurable, achievable, relevant, and time-bound (SMART). This framework helps individuals create actionable plans and track their progress, increasing the likelihood of success.

In addition to setting goals, developing grit involves cultivating a strong work ethic. This means being willing to put in the time and effort required to achieve one's objectives, even when the going gets tough. Gritty individuals understand that success is not achieved overnight; it requires consistent effort and dedication over the long term. By embracing hard work and persistence, individuals can build the grit needed to achieve their dreams.

Resilience and grit are also strengthened by building a supportive network of relationships. Having a strong support system provides individuals with encouragement, guidance, and accountability. Surrounding oneself with positive and like-minded individuals can inspire and motivate, creating an environment conducive to resilience and grit. Additionally, seeking mentorship from those who have overcome similar challenges can provide valuable insights and strategies for success.

Learning from failure is another important aspect of developing resilience and grit. Failure is an inevitable part of life, but it does not have to be a setback. Instead, it can be a valuable learning experience that provides insights and opportunities for growth. By analyzing failures and identifying lessons learned, individuals can develop the resilience and grit needed to persevere and achieve their goals.

Resilience and grit are not static qualities; they require ongoing effort and practice to maintain. This involves regularly challenging oneself and stepping outside of one's comfort zone. By taking on new challenges and pushing one's limits, individuals can build the resilience and grit needed to thrive in an ever-changing world.

Incorporating resilience and grit into daily life involves making intentional choices and adopting habits that reinforce these qualities. This may include setting aside time for self-reflection, practicing gratitude, and celebrating small victories along the way. By consistently nurturing resilience and grit, individuals can create a foundation for success and fulfillment.

Embracing Failure as a Learning Tool

Failure is often perceived as a negative outcome, a setback that hinders progress and diminishes self-worth. However, when viewed through a different lens, failure can be a powerful learning tool that fosters growth, innovation, and resilience. Embracing failure as an integral part of the learning process allows individuals to extract valuable insights and experiences that contribute to personal and professional development.

The fear of failure is deeply ingrained in many, stemming from societal pressures and the desire for success. This fear can lead to a reluctance to take risks or try new things, ultimately stifling creativity and innovation. By reframing failure as an opportunity for learning, individuals can overcome this fear and unlock their potential. This shift in perspective encourages a mindset that values experimentation and exploration, recognizing that failure is not the end, but rather a stepping stone toward success.

One of the key aspects of embracing failure is understanding that it is an inevitable part of any journey. Whether in personal endeavors or professional pursuits, setbacks and mistakes are bound to occur. Accepting this reality allows individuals to approach challenges with a sense of curiosity and openness, rather than apprehension. By acknowledging that failure is a natural part of the process, individuals can reduce the stigma associated with it and create an environment where learning and growth are prioritized.

To effectively use failure as a learning tool, it is essential to engage in reflective practice. This involves taking the time to analyze and evaluate the circumstances surrounding a failure, identifying the factors that contributed to the outcome, and considering alternative approaches. Reflective practice encourages critical thinking and self-awareness, enabling individuals to gain a deeper understanding of their actions and decisions. By systematically examining failures, individuals can uncover valuable lessons and insights that inform future endeavors.

Another important aspect of embracing failure is cultivating a growth mindset. This mindset, characterized by the belief that abilities and intelligence can be developed through effort and perseverance, is crucial for turning failure into a learning opportunity. Individuals with a growth mindset view challenges as opportunities for growth and are more likely to persist in the face of adversity. By adopting this mindset, individuals can approach failure with resilience and determination, using it as a catalyst for improvement and development.

Learning from failure also involves seeking feedback and input from others. Constructive feedback provides an external perspective that can shed light on blind spots and areas for improvement. By actively seeking feedback, individuals can gain valuable insights that may not be apparent from their own reflections. This collaborative approach to learning fosters a culture of openness and continuous improvement, where failure is seen as an opportunity for collective growth and development.

Incorporating failure into the learning process requires a willingness to take risks and step outside of one's comfort zone. This involves embracing uncertainty and being open to new experiences, even when the outcome is uncertain. By taking calculated risks and experimenting with different approaches, individuals can expand their horizons and discover new possibilities. This willingness to explore and innovate is essential for personal and professional growth, as it encourages adaptability and resilience in the face of change.

It is important to recognize that not all failures are created equal. Some failures may result from external factors beyond one's control, while others may be the result of poor planning or execution. Distinguishing between these types of failures is crucial for effective learning. While it is important to take responsibility for one's actions, it is equally important to recognize the limitations and constraints that may have contributed to the outcome. By understanding the context of a failure, individuals can develop more targeted strategies for improvement.

Embracing failure as a learning tool also involves celebrating small victories and progress along the way. Acknowledging and appreciating the incremental steps taken toward a goal can boost motivation and morale, reinforcing the value of persistence and effort. By focusing on progress rather than perfection, individuals can maintain a positive outlook and continue to strive for improvement, even in the face of setbacks.

Creating a supportive environment that encourages experimentation and learning from failure is essential for fostering a culture of growth and innovation. This involves promoting open communication, collaboration, and a willingness to share experiences and insights. By creating a safe space where failure is not stigmatized but embraced as a valuable learning opportunity, individuals can feel empowered to take risks and pursue their goals with confidence.

Strategies for Maintaining Mental Clarity

Mental clarity is an essential component of a fulfilling and productive life. It allows individuals to think clearly, make informed decisions, and navigate the complexities of daily life with ease. However, maintaining mental clarity can be challenging, especially in a world filled with distractions and stressors. By adopting effective strategies, individuals can enhance their mental clarity and improve their overall well-being.

One of the most effective strategies for maintaining mental clarity is establishing a consistent routine. A structured daily routine provides a sense of stability and predictability, reducing mental clutter and enhancing focus. By setting aside specific times for work, relaxation, and self-care, individuals can create a balanced lifestyle that supports mental clarity. This routine should include regular sleep patterns, as adequate rest is crucial for cognitive function and mental sharpness.

Mindfulness practices, such as meditation and deep breathing exercises, are powerful tools for enhancing mental clarity. These practices encourage individuals to focus on the present moment, reducing stress and anxiety that can cloud the mind. By incorporating mindfulness into daily life, individuals can cultivate a sense of calm and clarity, allowing them to approach challenges with a clear and focused mind. Even a few minutes of mindfulness practice each day can have a significant impact on mental clarity.

Physical activity is another important factor in maintaining mental clarity. Regular exercise has been shown to improve cognitive function, boost mood, and reduce stress. Engaging in physical activities, such as walking, jogging, or yoga, can help clear the mind and enhance focus. Exercise increases blood flow to the brain, promoting the release of endorphins and other chemicals that support mental clarity and well-being. Incorporating physical activity into daily routines can provide a natural and effective way to maintain mental clarity.

Nutrition also plays a critical role in mental clarity. A balanced diet that includes a variety of nutrients supports brain health and cognitive function. Foods rich in omega-3 fatty acids, antioxidants, and vitamins are particularly beneficial for mental clarity. Staying hydrated is equally important, as dehydration can lead to fatigue and impaired cognitive function. By prioritizing a healthy diet and staying hydrated, individuals can support their mental clarity and overall well-being.

Limiting exposure to digital distractions is essential for maintaining mental clarity. In today's digital age, constant notifications and information overload can lead to mental fatigue and reduced focus. Setting boundaries around technology use, such as designated screen-free times or digital detox days, can help reduce distractions and enhance mental clarity. Creating a designated workspace free from digital interruptions can also support focus and productivity.

Time management is a crucial skill for maintaining mental clarity. By prioritizing tasks and setting realistic goals, individuals can reduce stress and prevent mental overload. Breaking tasks into smaller, manageable steps can make them less daunting and more achievable. Utilizing tools such as planners or digital calendars can help individuals stay organized and focused, reducing mental clutter and enhancing clarity.

Social connections and support networks are vital for mental clarity. Engaging in meaningful interactions with friends, family, and colleagues can provide emotional support and reduce stress. Sharing experiences and seeking advice from others can offer new perspectives and insights, enhancing mental clarity. Building and maintaining strong social connections can create a sense of belonging and support, contributing to overall mental well-being.

Taking regular breaks and allowing time for relaxation is essential for maintaining mental clarity. Continuous work without breaks can lead to burnout and decreased cognitive function. Short breaks throughout the day can help refresh the mind and improve focus. Engaging in activities that promote relaxation, such as reading, listening to music, or spending time in nature, can provide a mental reset and enhance clarity.

Cultivating a positive mindset is another important strategy for maintaining mental clarity. Negative thoughts and self-doubt can cloud the mind and hinder decision-making. Practicing gratitude and focusing on positive aspects of life can shift perspective and enhance mental clarity. By challenging negative thoughts and reframing them in a positive light, individuals can foster a mindset that supports clarity and well-being.

Finally, seeking professional support when needed is an important aspect of maintaining mental clarity. Mental health professionals can provide guidance and support for individuals experiencing stress, anxiety, or other mental health challenges. Therapy or counseling can offer valuable tools and strategies for enhancing mental clarity and overall well-being. Recognizing when professional support is needed and taking proactive steps to seek help can make a significant difference in maintaining mental clarity.

Chapter 4

Creating a Motivating Environment

Designing a Space for Inspiration

Creating an environment that fosters inspiration is an art in itself. The spaces we inhabit have a profound impact on our creativity, productivity, and overall well-being. Designing a space that sparks inspiration involves a thoughtful blend of aesthetics, functionality, and personal expression. Whether it's a home office, a studio, or a cozy corner, the right environment can ignite the imagination and fuel the creative process.

The first step in designing an inspiring space is to consider its purpose. Understanding the activities that will take place in the space helps determine its layout and design elements. For instance, a writer's nook may require a comfortable chair and a desk with ample lighting, while an artist's studio might benefit from open space and natural light. Defining the purpose of the space ensures that it meets the specific needs of its user, creating an environment conducive to inspiration.

Color plays a significant role in shaping the mood and atmosphere of a space. Different colors evoke different emotions and can influence creativity in various ways. Soft blues and greens are known for their calming effects, promoting focus and tranquility. Vibrant hues like red and orange can energize and stimulate the mind, sparking creativity and enthusiasm. Choosing a color palette that resonates with personal preferences and the intended purpose of the space can enhance its inspirational qualities.

Lighting is another crucial element in designing a space for inspiration. Natural light is ideal, as it boosts mood and energy levels, creating a bright and inviting atmosphere. Positioning workspaces near windows or incorporating skylights can maximize exposure to natural light. In the absence of abundant natural light, a combination of ambient, task, and accent lighting can create a well-lit environment. Adjustable lighting options allow for flexibility, enabling individuals to tailor the lighting to their needs and preferences.

Furniture and layout are key considerations in creating an inspiring space. Comfortable and ergonomic furniture supports productivity and well-being, allowing individuals to focus on their creative endeavors. The layout should facilitate movement and flow, avoiding clutter and congestion.

Incorporating multifunctional furniture can optimize space and provide versatility, accommodating various activities and needs. Personal touches, such as artwork, plants, or decorative items, add character and warmth, making the space uniquely inspiring.

The use of textures and materials can enhance the sensory experience of a space, contributing to its inspirational qualities. Natural materials like wood, stone, and textiles create a sense of warmth and connection to nature. Incorporating a variety of textures, such as soft fabrics, smooth surfaces, and tactile elements, adds depth and interest to the space. These sensory elements can evoke emotions and memories, sparking creativity and inspiration.

Incorporating elements of nature into a space can have a profound impact on inspiration and well-being. Plants, flowers, and natural materials bring a sense of vitality and tranquility, connecting individuals to the natural world. Biophilic design, which emphasizes the integration of nature into built environments, has been shown to enhance creativity and reduce stress. Simple additions, such as potted plants, a small indoor garden, or nature-inspired artwork, can transform a space into a sanctuary of inspiration.

Personalization is a powerful tool in designing an inspiring space. Surrounding oneself with meaningful objects, mementos, and personal artifacts creates a sense of identity and connection. These items can serve as reminders of past achievements, aspirations, or sources of inspiration. A vision board, for example, can display images and quotes that resonate with personal goals and dreams. Personalization infuses the space with individuality, making it a reflection of one's unique creative journey.

Technology can be both a boon and a bane in an inspiring space. While it offers tools and resources that enhance creativity, it can also be a source of distraction. Striking a balance between technology and mindfulness is essential. Designating specific areas for technology use and incorporating digital detox zones can help maintain focus and inspiration. Utilizing technology mindfully, such as using apps for meditation or creative brainstorming, can enhance the inspirational qualities of the space.

Flexibility and adaptability are important considerations in designing a space for inspiration. Creative needs and preferences may evolve over time, and the space should be able to accommodate these changes. Modular furniture, movable partitions, and adjustable lighting allow for easy reconfiguration, enabling individuals to adapt the space to their current needs. A flexible space encourages experimentation and exploration, fostering a dynamic and inspiring environment.

Finally, maintaining an inspiring space requires regular attention and care. Keeping the space organized and clutter-free promotes clarity and focus, allowing inspiration to flow freely. Regularly refreshing the space with new elements, such as artwork, plants, or decor, can keep it vibrant and engaging. Taking the time to reflect on the space's effectiveness and making adjustments as needed ensures that it continues to inspire and support creative endeavors.

The Influence of Social Circles on Motivation

Social circles wield a profound influence on motivation, shaping our aspirations, behaviors, and ultimately, our success. The people we surround ourselves with can either propel us toward our goals or hinder our progress. Understanding the dynamics of social circles and their impact on motivation is crucial for anyone seeking to harness the power of social influence to achieve personal and professional growth.

At the heart of social influence lies the concept of social comparison. Humans have an innate tendency to evaluate themselves in relation to others, a process that can significantly affect motivation. When individuals compare themselves to those who are more successful or accomplished, it can inspire them to strive for similar achievements. This upward comparison can serve as a powerful motivator, pushing individuals to set higher goals and work diligently to attain them. Conversely, comparing oneself to those perceived as less successful can lead to complacency and a lack of motivation, as the perceived benchmark for success is lowered.

The role of social support in motivation cannot be overstated. A supportive social circle provides encouragement, validation, and assistance, fostering a sense of belonging and confidence. When individuals feel supported by their peers, they are more likely to take risks, pursue challenging goals, and persevere in the face of setbacks. Social support acts as a buffer against stress and adversity, enhancing resilience and motivation. In contrast, a lack of support or negative social interactions can undermine motivation, leading to self-doubt and disengagement.

Peer pressure, often perceived negatively, can also have a positive impact on motivation. When harnessed constructively, peer pressure can encourage individuals to adopt beneficial behaviors and attitudes. For example, being part of a group that values hard work and achievement can motivate individuals to align their actions with these values. The desire to gain acceptance and approval from one's social circle can drive individuals to push their limits and achieve their goals. However, it is essential to be mindful of the potential for negative peer pressure, which can lead to harmful behaviors and decreased motivation.

The concept of social identity plays a significant role in shaping motivation. Individuals derive a sense of identity and self-worth from their social groups, influencing their goals and aspirations. When individuals identify strongly with a group that values achievement and success, they are more likely to internalize these values and pursue related goals. Social identity can provide a sense of purpose and direction, motivating individuals to work toward goals that align with their group's values. On the other hand, identifying with a group that lacks ambition or direction can lead to stagnation and a lack of motivation.

Mentorship and role models within social circles can have a profound impact on motivation. Mentors provide guidance, support, and inspiration, helping individuals navigate challenges and achieve their goals. A mentor's belief in an individual's potential can boost confidence and motivation, encouraging them to pursue ambitious goals. Role models, whether within one's social circle or in the broader community, serve as examples of success and achievement. Observing the accomplishments of role models can inspire individuals to emulate their behaviors and strive for similar success.

The diversity of a social circle can also influence motivation. Exposure to diverse perspectives, experiences, and ideas can stimulate creativity and innovation, enhancing motivation. A diverse social circle can challenge individuals to think critically, question assumptions, and explore new possibilities. This exposure to different viewpoints can broaden horizons and inspire individuals to pursue goals they may not have considered otherwise. Conversely, a homogenous social circle can lead to conformity and limited thinking, stifling motivation and growth.

The size of a social circle can impact motivation in various ways. A larger social circle may provide access to a broader range of resources, opportunities, and support, enhancing motivation. However, it can also lead to increased social comparison and pressure, which may have negative effects on motivation. A smaller social circle may offer more intimate and supportive relationships, fostering a strong sense of belonging and motivation. Balancing the size and composition of one's social circle is essential for optimizing its influence on motivation.

Technology and social media have transformed the way social circles influence motivation. Online platforms provide access to a vast network of connections, enabling individuals to seek inspiration, support, and guidance from a global community. Social media can serve as a source of motivation by showcasing success stories, sharing knowledge, and fostering a sense of community. However, it can also lead to negative social comparison and pressure, as individuals are exposed to curated and idealized portrayals of others' lives. Navigating the digital landscape mindfully is crucial for harnessing its motivational potential while mitigating its drawbacks.

Cultivating a social circle that positively influences motivation requires intentionality and discernment. Building relationships with individuals who share similar values, goals, and aspirations can create a supportive and motivating environment. Engaging in activities and communities that align with one's interests and passions can facilitate the formation of meaningful connections. It is also important to evaluate and, if necessary, distance oneself from relationships that have a negative impact on motivation and well-being.

Utilizing Technology to Stay Motivated

Technology has become an integral part of our daily lives, offering a myriad of tools and resources to help us stay motivated and achieve our goals. From productivity apps to online communities, technology provides innovative ways to enhance motivation and maintain focus. Understanding how to effectively utilize these technological resources can empower individuals to harness their full potential and stay on track in their personal and professional endeavors.

One of the most significant ways technology aids motivation is through the use of productivity apps. These applications are designed to help individuals organize their tasks, set goals, and track progress. By breaking down larger goals into manageable tasks, productivity apps can reduce feelings of overwhelm and increase motivation. Features such as reminders, deadlines, and progress tracking provide a sense of accountability and accomplishment, encouraging individuals to stay committed to their goals. Popular productivity apps like Todoist, Trello, and Asana offer customizable interfaces that cater to different preferences and work styles, making it easier for users to find a system that works for them.

In addition to productivity apps, technology offers a wealth of resources for learning and skill development. Online courses, tutorials, and webinars provide opportunities for individuals to acquire new knowledge and skills, fueling motivation by fostering a sense of growth and achievement. Platforms like Coursera, Udemy, and Khan Academy offer a diverse range of courses, allowing individuals to pursue their interests and passions at their own pace. The accessibility of online learning resources enables individuals to continuously challenge themselves and expand their horizons, keeping motivation levels high.

Virtual communities and social networks play a crucial role in maintaining motivation by providing support, encouragement, and inspiration. Online forums, groups, and social media platforms connect individuals with like-minded peers who share similar goals and interests. These virtual communities offer a space for individuals to share experiences, seek advice, and celebrate achievements, fostering a sense of camaraderie and belonging. The encouragement and validation received from online communities can boost motivation and confidence, helping individuals stay committed to their goals. Platforms like Reddit, Facebook groups, and LinkedIn offer diverse communities catering to various interests and professional fields.

Gamification is another powerful tool that technology offers to enhance motivation. By incorporating game-like elements such as rewards, challenges, and leaderboards, gamification can make tasks more engaging and enjoyable. This approach taps into the human desire for achievement and competition, motivating individuals to complete

tasks and reach milestones. Apps like Habitica and
Forest use gamification to encourage users to
develop positive habits and stay focused on their
goals. By transforming mundane tasks into exciting
challenges, gamification can increase motivation and
productivity.

Mindfulness and meditation apps provide valuable
resources for maintaining motivation by promoting
mental well-being and focus. These apps offer
guided meditations, breathing exercises, and
relaxation techniques that help individuals manage
stress and maintain a positive mindset. By fostering a
sense of calm and clarity, mindfulness apps can
enhance motivation by improving concentration and
reducing distractions. Popular mindfulness apps like
Headspace and Calm offer a variety of programs
tailored to different needs and preferences, making it
easier for individuals to incorporate mindfulness
practices into their daily routines.

Technology also offers tools for tracking and
analyzing personal data, providing insights that can
enhance motivation. Fitness trackers, for example,
monitor physical activity, sleep patterns, and other
health metrics, offering a comprehensive view of
one's well-being. By setting fitness goals and tracking
progress, individuals can stay motivated to maintain
a healthy lifestyle. Similarly, apps that track habits,
moods, and productivity can provide valuable

insights into patterns and behaviors, helping individuals identify areas for improvement and set realistic goals. The data-driven approach offered by these tools can increase motivation by providing tangible evidence of progress and achievement.

The integration of virtual reality (VR) and augmented reality (AR) into motivational tools offers exciting possibilities for enhancing motivation. VR and AR technologies create immersive experiences that can make learning and goal-setting more engaging and interactive. For example, VR fitness apps provide virtual environments that make exercise more enjoyable and motivating. AR applications can overlay digital information onto the real world, offering interactive learning experiences that enhance motivation and retention. As VR and AR technologies continue to evolve, their potential to boost motivation and engagement will only increase.

While technology offers numerous benefits for staying motivated, it is essential to be mindful of potential pitfalls. The constant connectivity and information overload that technology provides can lead to distractions and decreased motivation. Setting boundaries and establishing healthy technology habits is crucial for maintaining focus and motivation. Techniques such as digital detoxes, time management strategies, and mindful technology use can help individuals strike a balance between leveraging technology for motivation and avoiding its potential drawbacks.

The Importance of Routine and Structure

The gentle hum of a bustling city, the rhythmic tapping of fingers on keyboards, and the soft glow of screens illuminating faces—these are the sights and sounds of a world deeply intertwined with technology. In this digital age, technology is not merely a tool but a companion, guiding us through the labyrinth of daily life. It offers a plethora of resources to keep us motivated, driven, and focused on our aspirations. Understanding how to harness these technological marvels can transform our approach to motivation, turning challenges into opportunities for growth and achievement.

Imagine waking up to the gentle chime of an alarm that not only rouses you from slumber but also greets you with a curated list of tasks for the day. Productivity apps have revolutionized the way we organize our lives, offering features that break down daunting goals into manageable tasks. These digital assistants provide reminders, set deadlines, and track progress, creating a sense of accountability that fuels motivation. The satisfaction of checking off completed tasks is a powerful motivator, instilling a sense of accomplishment that propels us forward. Apps like Todoist and Trello cater to diverse preferences, allowing users to customize their interfaces and find a system that resonates with their unique work style.

Beyond organization, technology opens doors to a world of knowledge and skill development. Online courses and tutorials offer a treasure trove of learning opportunities, empowering individuals to acquire new skills and expand their horizons. Platforms such as Coursera and Udemy provide access to a vast array of subjects, enabling learners to pursue their passions at their own pace. The ability to learn from experts across the globe fosters a sense of growth and achievement, keeping motivation levels high. This continuous pursuit of knowledge not only enhances personal development but also instills a sense of purpose and direction.

In the realm of motivation, the power of community cannot be underestimated. Virtual communities and social networks connect individuals with like-minded peers, creating spaces for support, encouragement, and inspiration. Online forums and social media platforms offer a sense of camaraderie, where individuals can share experiences, seek advice, and celebrate achievements. The validation and encouragement received from these communities boost confidence and motivation, reinforcing the commitment to personal goals. Platforms like Reddit and Facebook groups host diverse communities that cater to various interests, providing a sense of belonging and shared purpose.

Gamification, the art of incorporating game-like elements into non-game contexts, has emerged as a potent motivator. By introducing rewards, challenges, and leaderboards, gamification transforms mundane tasks into engaging experiences. This approach taps into the human desire for achievement and competition, motivating individuals to reach milestones and complete tasks. Apps like Habitica and Forest utilize gamification to encourage users to develop positive habits and maintain focus. By turning everyday tasks into exciting challenges, gamification enhances motivation and productivity, making goal attainment an enjoyable journey.

Mindfulness and meditation apps offer a sanctuary for mental well-being, promoting focus and motivation through relaxation techniques. These apps provide guided meditations and breathing exercises that help individuals manage stress and maintain a positive mindset. By fostering a sense of calm and clarity, mindfulness practices enhance concentration and reduce distractions, bolstering motivation. Popular apps like Headspace and Calm offer a variety of programs tailored to different needs, making it easy to incorporate mindfulness into daily routines. This mental fortitude is crucial for maintaining motivation, as it empowers individuals to navigate challenges with resilience and determination.

The advent of wearable technology has introduced a new dimension to motivation, offering tools for tracking and analyzing personal data. Fitness trackers monitor physical activity, sleep patterns, and health metrics, providing insights that inform lifestyle choices. By setting fitness goals and tracking progress, individuals can stay motivated to maintain a healthy lifestyle. Similarly, apps that track habits and productivity offer valuable insights into patterns and behaviors, helping individuals identify areas for improvement. This data-driven approach provides tangible evidence of progress, reinforcing motivation and commitment to personal goals.

Virtual reality (VR) and augmented reality (AR) technologies offer immersive experiences that enhance motivation through interactive learning and goal-setting. VR fitness apps create virtual environments that make exercise enjoyable and engaging, while AR applications overlay digital information onto the real world, offering interactive learning experiences. These technologies captivate the senses, making motivation an experiential journey. As VR and AR continue to evolve, their potential to boost motivation and engagement will only grow, offering exciting possibilities for personal and professional development.

While technology offers a wealth of resources for motivation, it is essential to navigate its potential pitfalls. The constant connectivity and information overload can lead to distractions and decreased motivation. Establishing healthy technology habits and setting boundaries is crucial for maintaining focus. Techniques such as digital detoxes and mindful technology use can help individuals strike a balance between leveraging technology for motivation and avoiding its drawbacks. By approaching technology with intentionality and discernment, individuals can harness its power to stay motivated and achieve their goals.

Minimizing Distractions and Enhancing Focus

The modern world is a cacophony of distractions, each vying for attention with relentless persistence. From the incessant ping of notifications to the allure of social media, maintaining focus has become a formidable challenge. Yet, in this whirlwind of stimuli, the ability to concentrate remains a crucial skill, one that can significantly impact productivity and personal fulfillment. Understanding how to minimize distractions and enhance focus is essential for navigating the demands of contemporary life.

Picture a serene morning, the sun casting gentle rays through the window as you settle into your workspace. The day holds promise, yet the digital world beckons with its myriad temptations. The first step in cultivating focus is creating an environment conducive to concentration. This involves both physical and digital decluttering. A tidy workspace, free from unnecessary items, can reduce visual distractions and promote a sense of calm. Similarly, organizing digital devices by closing irrelevant tabs and silencing non-essential notifications can help maintain mental clarity.

Establishing a routine is another powerful strategy for enhancing focus. By setting specific times for work, breaks, and leisure, you create a rhythm that trains the mind to concentrate during designated periods. This routine acts as a signal to the brain, indicating when it's time to focus and when it's time to relax. Consistency in routine fosters discipline, making it easier to resist distractions and maintain concentration over time. Incorporating rituals, such as a morning meditation or a brief walk, can further reinforce this routine, providing a mental reset that enhances focus.

The Pomodoro Technique, a time management method developed by Francesco Cirillo, offers a structured approach to maintaining focus. By breaking work into intervals, typically 25 minutes in length, followed by short breaks, this technique capitalizes on the brain's natural attention span. These intervals, known as "Pomodoros," create a sense of urgency that encourages concentration, while the breaks provide an opportunity to recharge. This cyclical pattern of work and rest helps prevent burnout and maintains sustained focus throughout the day.

Mindfulness practices, such as meditation and deep breathing exercises, can also play a pivotal role in enhancing focus. By training the mind to remain present and aware, mindfulness reduces the tendency to become distracted by external stimuli or wandering thoughts. Regular mindfulness practice strengthens the brain's ability to concentrate, making it easier to stay focused on tasks. Techniques such as mindful breathing or body scans can be incorporated into daily routines, providing moments of calm that enhance overall concentration.

The digital age has introduced a plethora of tools designed to combat distractions and promote focus. Applications that block distracting websites or limit screen time can be invaluable allies in the quest for concentration. These tools create a digital barrier, preventing the temptation to stray from tasks and ensuring that focus remains unbroken. By setting boundaries on digital consumption, individuals can reclaim control over their attention and direct it towards meaningful pursuits.

Physical well-being is intrinsically linked to mental focus. Adequate sleep, regular exercise, and a balanced diet are foundational elements that support cognitive function and concentration. Sleep, in particular, plays a critical role in memory consolidation and mental clarity. Ensuring sufficient rest enhances the brain's ability to process information and maintain focus. Similarly, physical activity increases blood flow to the brain, boosting cognitive performance and reducing stress. A nutritious diet, rich in brain-boosting nutrients, provides the energy needed for sustained concentration.

The power of intention should not be underestimated when it comes to minimizing distractions. Setting clear, specific goals for each task provides a roadmap that guides focus and effort. By defining what needs to be accomplished and why, individuals can align their actions with their objectives, reducing the likelihood of succumbing to distractions. This intentionality creates a sense of purpose that fuels motivation and concentration, making it easier to stay on track.

Social accountability can also enhance focus by introducing an element of external motivation. Sharing goals with a friend or colleague creates a sense of responsibility, as the desire to meet expectations can drive concentration. Regular check-ins or progress updates provide opportunities for reflection and adjustment, ensuring that focus remains aligned with objectives. This collaborative approach fosters a supportive environment that encourages sustained concentration and achievement.

In the quest to minimize distractions, it is important to recognize the role of self-compassion. The journey to enhanced focus is not without its challenges, and setbacks are a natural part of the process. Embracing these moments with kindness and understanding allows individuals to learn from their experiences and continue striving for improvement. By acknowledging the ebb and flow of concentration, individuals can cultivate resilience and perseverance, essential qualities for maintaining focus in a world filled with distractions.

Chapter 5

Techniques to Boost Motivation

Visualization and Affirmations

The mind is a powerful tool, capable of shaping reality through the thoughts and beliefs it harbors. Visualization and affirmations are two techniques that harness this power, enabling individuals to manifest their desires and achieve their goals. By creating vivid mental images and reinforcing positive beliefs, these practices can transform aspirations into tangible outcomes.

Imagine standing at the edge of a vast ocean, the horizon stretching endlessly before you. The waves crash rhythmically against the shore, each one a reminder of the boundless potential that lies within. Visualization is akin to this ocean, a limitless expanse where dreams take form and possibilities unfold. It involves creating detailed mental images of desired outcomes, engaging all the senses to make these images as vivid and real as possible. This mental rehearsal primes the brain for success, activating neural pathways associated with the envisioned scenario.

The process of visualization begins with clarity. Identifying specific goals and outcomes is essential, as it provides a clear target for the mind to focus on. Once the goal is defined, the next step is to create a mental image that encapsulates this desired outcome. This image should be rich in detail, incorporating sights, sounds, smells, and emotions associated with the achievement. By immersing oneself in this mental scene, the brain begins to perceive it as reality, increasing motivation and confidence.

Visualization is not limited to static images; it can also involve dynamic scenarios that unfold over time. For instance, an athlete might visualize the entire sequence of a race, from the starting gun to crossing the finish line. This dynamic visualization allows the mind to rehearse complex actions and responses, enhancing performance and reducing anxiety. By repeatedly visualizing success, individuals can build a mental blueprint that guides their actions and decisions in the real world.

Affirmations complement visualization by reinforcing positive beliefs and attitudes. These are short, powerful statements that declare a desired state or outcome as if it is already true. By repeating affirmations regularly, individuals can reprogram their subconscious mind, replacing limiting beliefs with empowering ones. This shift in mindset can have a profound impact on behavior and outcomes, as beliefs shape actions and actions shape reality.

Crafting effective affirmations requires careful consideration of language and intent. Affirmations should be positive, present-tense, and specific, focusing on what is desired rather than what is lacking. For example, instead of saying "I will not fail," an affirmation might be "I am successful in all my endeavors." This positive framing directs the mind towards success, fostering a sense of confidence and self-efficacy.

The repetition of affirmations is key to their effectiveness. By consistently repeating these statements, ideally in a relaxed and focused state, individuals can embed them into their subconscious mind. This repetition creates new neural pathways, reinforcing the belief and making it a part of one's identity. Over time, these ingrained beliefs influence thoughts, emotions, and actions, aligning them with the desired outcome.

Combining visualization and affirmations creates a powerful synergy that amplifies their effects. Visualization provides a vivid mental image of success, while affirmations reinforce the belief that this success is attainable. Together, they create a mental environment that supports goal achievement, fostering a mindset of possibility and abundance.

The practice of visualization and affirmations is not limited to personal goals; it can also be applied to professional and creative pursuits. Artists, writers, and entrepreneurs often use these techniques to overcome creative blocks and manifest their visions. By visualizing the completion of a project or the realization of an idea, they can tap into their creative potential and bring their aspirations to life.

Incorporating visualization and affirmations into daily routines can enhance their effectiveness. Setting aside dedicated time each day for these practices creates a habit that reinforces positive thinking and goal orientation. This routine can be as simple as spending a few minutes each morning visualizing the day's goals and repeating affirmations. Over time, this consistent practice can lead to significant shifts in mindset and outcomes.

The power of visualization and affirmations lies in their ability to align the mind with desired outcomes. By creating a mental landscape of success and reinforcing positive beliefs, individuals can navigate the challenges of life with confidence and clarity. These practices serve as a reminder of the limitless potential that resides within, waiting to be harnessed and directed towards meaningful pursuits.

The Role of Rewards and Incentives

Rewards and incentives play a pivotal role in shaping behavior and driving motivation. They serve as powerful tools that can influence actions, reinforce positive behavior, and encourage the pursuit of goals. Understanding the dynamics of rewards and incentives is crucial for anyone seeking to harness their potential, whether in personal development, education, or the workplace.

Imagine a child eagerly anticipating a gold star for completing their homework. This simple reward can transform a mundane task into an exciting challenge. The anticipation of a reward activates the brain's pleasure centers, releasing dopamine, a neurotransmitter associated with motivation and pleasure. This chemical response not only makes the task more enjoyable but also reinforces the behavior, making it more likely to be repeated in the future.

In the realm of personal development, rewards and incentives can be strategically employed to cultivate habits and achieve goals. Setting up a system of rewards for reaching milestones can provide the motivation needed to persevere through challenges. For instance, someone aiming to improve their fitness might reward themselves with a new workout outfit after reaching a certain number of workouts.

This tangible reward serves as a reminder of progress and an incentive to continue striving towards the ultimate goal.

The effectiveness of rewards and incentives is not limited to tangible items; intangible rewards can be equally powerful. Praise, recognition, and a sense of accomplishment are all forms of intangible rewards that can significantly impact motivation. In a workplace setting, acknowledging an employee's hard work with verbal recognition can boost morale and encourage continued effort. This type of reward fosters a positive work environment and reinforces the value of the employee's contributions.

However, the use of rewards and incentives requires careful consideration to avoid potential pitfalls. Over-reliance on external rewards can lead to a phenomenon known as the overjustification effect, where intrinsic motivation diminishes as individuals become dependent on external incentives. To mitigate this risk, it's important to strike a balance between extrinsic and intrinsic motivation. Encouraging individuals to find personal meaning and satisfaction in their tasks can help maintain intrinsic motivation while still benefiting from the motivational boost provided by rewards.

In educational settings, rewards and incentives can be powerful motivators for students. Teachers often use a variety of reward systems, such as stickers, certificates, or extra recess time, to encourage positive behavior and academic achievement. These incentives can create a positive learning environment where students feel motivated to participate and excel. However, it's essential to ensure that rewards are used to enhance learning rather than replace it. Encouraging a love for learning and curiosity should remain the primary focus, with rewards serving as supplementary motivators.

The role of rewards and incentives extends beyond individual motivation; they can also influence group dynamics and organizational culture. In a team setting, collective rewards can foster collaboration and a sense of shared purpose. For example, a team might be rewarded with a group outing or a celebratory lunch after successfully completing a project. This type of reward not only acknowledges the team's hard work but also strengthens bonds and encourages future collaboration.

Incentive programs in organizations can drive performance and productivity by aligning individual goals with organizational objectives. Performance-based bonuses, profit-sharing, and recognition programs are common examples of incentives used to motivate employees. These programs can create a culture of excellence, where employees are motivated to contribute their best efforts to achieve both personal and organizational success.

Designing effective reward and incentive systems requires a deep understanding of human motivation and behavior. It's important to tailor rewards to the preferences and values of the individuals or groups involved. What motivates one person may not necessarily motivate another, so personalization is key. Additionally, the timing and frequency of rewards can impact their effectiveness. Immediate rewards can provide instant gratification and reinforce behavior, while delayed rewards can build anticipation and encourage long-term commitment.

The role of rewards and incentives is not static; it evolves as individuals and organizations grow and change. Regularly assessing and adjusting reward systems ensures they remain relevant and effective. Feedback from participants can provide valuable insights into what works and what doesn't, allowing for continuous improvement.

Time Management for Maximum Productivity

Time management is an essential skill that can significantly enhance productivity and efficiency in both personal and professional life. The ability to effectively manage time allows individuals to accomplish more in less time, reduce stress, and achieve a better work-life balance. By understanding and implementing key time management strategies, one can unlock their full potential and make the most of each day.

Consider the story of Sarah, a young professional juggling multiple responsibilities at work and home. She often found herself overwhelmed, struggling to meet deadlines, and sacrificing personal time to catch up on tasks. Determined to regain control, Sarah embarked on a journey to master time management. Her transformation began with a simple yet powerful tool: the to-do list. By writing down tasks and prioritizing them, she gained clarity on what needed to be done and when. This practice not only helped her stay organized but also provided a sense of accomplishment as she checked off completed tasks.

Prioritization is a cornerstone of effective time management. It involves distinguishing between tasks that are urgent and those that are important. The Eisenhower Matrix, a popular prioritization tool, categorizes tasks into four quadrants: urgent and important, important but not urgent, urgent but not important, and neither urgent nor important. By focusing on tasks that are both urgent and important, individuals can ensure that critical responsibilities are addressed promptly, while also allocating time for important but less urgent activities that contribute to long-term goals.

Another key aspect of time management is setting realistic goals. Goals provide direction and motivation, but they must be achievable within the available time frame. Breaking down larger goals into smaller, manageable tasks can make them less daunting and more attainable. This approach not only prevents procrastination but also allows for steady progress, as each completed task brings one closer to the ultimate objective.

Time blocking is a technique that involves allocating specific blocks of time for different activities throughout the day. By dedicating uninterrupted time to focus on a single task, individuals can minimize distractions and enhance concentration. This method is particularly effective for tasks that require deep focus and creativity. For instance, a writer might set aside a two-hour block each morning for writing, free from interruptions, to maximize productivity and maintain a steady flow of ideas.

The Pomodoro Technique is another popular time management strategy that can boost productivity. It involves working in short, focused bursts of 25 minutes, followed by a five-minute break. After completing four such cycles, a longer break of 15 to 30 minutes is taken. This technique leverages the brain's natural attention span, preventing burnout and maintaining high levels of focus and energy throughout the day.

Delegation is a powerful tool for managing time effectively, especially in a professional setting. By entrusting tasks to others, individuals can free up time to focus on high-priority responsibilities that require their unique skills and expertise. Effective delegation involves clear communication, setting expectations, and providing the necessary resources and support to ensure successful task completion. This not only enhances productivity but also fosters a collaborative work environment where team members feel valued and empowered.

Technology can be both a boon and a bane when it comes to time management. While digital tools and apps can streamline tasks and improve efficiency, they can also be a source of distraction. To harness the benefits of technology, it's important to set boundaries and establish tech-free zones or times. For example, turning off notifications during focused work sessions can minimize interruptions and help maintain concentration. Additionally, using productivity apps to track time, set reminders, and organize tasks can provide valuable insights into how time is spent and identify areas for improvement.

Self-discipline and accountability are crucial components of successful time management. Developing self-discipline involves cultivating habits that support productivity, such as starting the day with a clear plan, minimizing procrastination, and adhering to set schedules. Accountability, whether through self-monitoring or involving others, can provide the motivation needed to stay on track. Sharing goals with a colleague or friend and regularly updating them on progress can create a sense of responsibility and encourage consistent effort.

Reflecting on and evaluating time management practices is essential for continuous improvement. Regularly reviewing how time is allocated and identifying patterns or habits that hinder productivity can lead to valuable insights and adjustments. This process of reflection allows individuals to refine their strategies, adapt to changing circumstances, and ultimately achieve greater efficiency and effectiveness.

Mindfulness and Meditation Practices

Mindfulness and meditation have become increasingly popular as tools for enhancing mental well-being and fostering a deeper connection with oneself. These practices, rooted in ancient traditions, offer a pathway to greater awareness, emotional balance, and inner peace. By incorporating mindfulness and meditation into daily life, individuals can cultivate a more present and intentional existence, ultimately leading to a more fulfilling and harmonious life.

Imagine a bustling city, where the noise of traffic and the constant hum of activity create a backdrop of chaos. Amidst this whirlwind, there is a small park, a sanctuary of calm and tranquility. This park represents the essence of mindfulness—a space within the mind where one can retreat from the noise and find stillness. Mindfulness is the practice of being fully present in the moment, without judgment or distraction. It involves observing thoughts, emotions, and sensations with curiosity and acceptance, allowing them to come and go without attachment.

One of the simplest ways to begin practicing mindfulness is through mindful breathing. This technique involves focusing attention on the breath, noticing the sensation of air entering and leaving the body. By anchoring awareness to the breath, individuals can quiet the mind and cultivate a sense of calm. Mindful breathing can be practiced anywhere, at any time, making it a versatile tool for managing stress and enhancing focus.

Body scan meditation is another effective mindfulness practice that promotes relaxation and body awareness. This technique involves mentally scanning the body from head to toe, observing any areas of tension or discomfort. By bringing attention to each part of the body, individuals can release physical tension and develop a greater sense of connection with their physical selves. This practice not only enhances relaxation but also fosters a deeper understanding of the mind-body connection.

Loving-kindness meditation, also known as Metta meditation, is a practice that cultivates compassion and empathy. It involves silently repeating phrases of goodwill and kindness, first towards oneself and then extending these sentiments to others. This practice can help individuals develop a more compassionate and empathetic outlook, reducing feelings of anger and resentment. By fostering a sense of interconnectedness, loving-kindness meditation can enhance relationships and promote a more harmonious existence.

Mindful walking is a practice that combines movement with mindfulness, offering an opportunity to connect with the present moment while engaging in physical activity. During mindful walking, individuals focus on the sensations of each step, the rhythm of their breath, and the environment around them. This practice encourages a deeper appreciation of the present moment and can transform a routine walk into a meditative experience.

Meditation, a complementary practice to mindfulness, involves setting aside dedicated time to cultivate a focused and relaxed state of mind. There are various forms of meditation, each with its unique approach and benefits. One popular form is transcendental meditation, which involves silently repeating a mantra to settle the mind into a state of profound rest and relaxation. This practice can reduce stress, enhance creativity, and promote overall well-being.

Guided meditation is another accessible form of meditation, particularly for beginners. It involves listening to a recorded meditation session led by an experienced practitioner, who provides instructions and guidance throughout the practice. Guided meditations can focus on various themes, such as relaxation, gratitude, or self-compassion, allowing individuals to explore different aspects of their inner world.

Mindfulness and meditation practices offer numerous benefits, both mental and physical. Regular practice can reduce stress, anxiety, and depression, while also improving focus, concentration, and emotional regulation. These practices can enhance self-awareness, allowing individuals to gain insight into their thoughts, emotions, and behaviors. By fostering a greater sense of presence and acceptance, mindfulness and meditation can lead to a more balanced and fulfilling life.

Incorporating mindfulness and meditation into daily life requires commitment and consistency. It is important to set aside dedicated time for practice, whether it be a few minutes each day or longer sessions on a regular basis. Creating a designated space for practice, free from distractions, can also enhance the experience. Additionally, approaching these practices with an open mind and a sense of curiosity can lead to deeper insights and personal growth.

Harnessing the Power of Music and Art

Music and art have long been celebrated as powerful mediums of expression, capable of transcending language and cultural barriers. They possess the unique ability to evoke emotions, inspire creativity, and foster a sense of connection among individuals. By harnessing the power of music and art, one can unlock new dimensions of personal growth, emotional healing, and social engagement.

Consider the scene of a bustling city street, where the cacophony of honking cars and hurried footsteps is suddenly interrupted by the soulful notes of a street musician's violin. In that moment, the music creates a shared experience, drawing strangers together in a collective pause. This illustrates the profound impact music can have on our lives, offering solace and connection in an often chaotic world.

Music has the ability to influence our emotions and mental states in profound ways. Listening to a favorite song can evoke memories, uplift spirits, or provide comfort during difficult times. Research has shown that music can reduce stress, alleviate anxiety, and even improve cognitive function. By incorporating music into daily routines, individuals can enhance their emotional well-being and create a more harmonious environment.

Creating music, whether through playing an instrument or composing original pieces, offers an opportunity for self-expression and personal exploration. It allows individuals to communicate emotions and ideas that may be difficult to articulate through words alone. Engaging in musical activities can also foster a sense of accomplishment and boost self-esteem, as individuals develop new skills and achieve creative goals.

Art, like music, serves as a powerful tool for self-expression and emotional exploration. Whether through painting, drawing, sculpture, or other forms, art provides a visual language through which individuals can convey their innermost thoughts and feelings. The act of creating art can be therapeutic, offering a means of processing emotions and experiences in a tangible way.

Art can also serve as a catalyst for social change, challenging perceptions and sparking important conversations. Throughout history, artists have used their work to address social and political issues, raising awareness and inspiring action. By engaging with art, individuals can gain new perspectives and develop a deeper understanding of the world around them.

Incorporating art into daily life can enhance creativity and foster a sense of mindfulness. Engaging in artistic activities encourages individuals to slow down, observe their surroundings, and appreciate the beauty in everyday moments. This practice can lead to greater self-awareness and a more intentional way of living.

For those seeking to harness the power of music and art, there are numerous ways to begin. Attending live performances, visiting art galleries, or participating in workshops can provide inspiration and exposure to new ideas. Exploring different genres of music and styles of art can broaden one's horizons and deepen appreciation for diverse forms of expression.

Creating a dedicated space for music and art in the home can also enhance the experience. This space can serve as a sanctuary for creative exploration, free from distractions and interruptions. By setting aside time for regular practice, individuals can cultivate their skills and develop a deeper connection with their chosen medium.

Collaboration is another powerful aspect of music and art, offering opportunities for shared creativity and mutual inspiration. Joining a band, choir, or art collective can foster a sense of community and provide valuable feedback and support. Collaborative projects can also lead to innovative ideas and new approaches, as individuals draw on each other's strengths and perspectives.

The digital age has opened up new avenues for accessing and sharing music and art. Online platforms and social media provide opportunities for artists and musicians to reach wider audiences and connect with like-minded individuals. By leveraging these tools, individuals can share their work, gain exposure, and engage with a global community of creators.

Mindfulness and Motivation

Mindfulness and motivation are two powerful forces that, when combined, can significantly enhance personal and professional growth. Mindfulness, the practice of being fully present and aware in the moment, can serve as a catalyst for motivation by fostering clarity, focus, and emotional balance. Understanding how these two elements interact can lead to a more fulfilling and productive life.

At the heart of mindfulness is the ability to observe one's thoughts and emotions without judgment. This non-reactive awareness allows individuals to gain insight into their motivations and desires. By understanding the underlying reasons for their actions, people can align their goals with their true values and passions. This alignment creates a sense of purpose and direction, which is a key driver of motivation. When individuals are clear about what they want and why they want it, they are more likely to pursue their goals with enthusiasm and determination.

Mindfulness also enhances motivation by reducing stress and anxiety. When the mind is cluttered with worries and distractions, it becomes difficult to focus on tasks and maintain motivation. Mindfulness practices, such as meditation and deep breathing, help to calm the mind and create a sense of inner peace. This mental clarity allows individuals to concentrate on their goals and take purposeful action. By cultivating a calm and focused mind, individuals can overcome obstacles and stay motivated even in challenging situations.

Another way mindfulness boosts motivation is by increasing self-awareness. Through mindfulness, individuals become more attuned to their thoughts, emotions, and physical sensations. This heightened awareness enables them to recognize patterns of behavior that may be hindering their motivation. For example, they may notice that negative self-talk or fear of failure is holding them back. By identifying these barriers, individuals can take steps to address them and cultivate a more positive and motivated mindset.

Mindfulness encourages a growth mindset, which is essential for sustained motivation. A growth mindset is the belief that abilities and intelligence can be developed through effort and learning. Mindfulness fosters this mindset by promoting curiosity and openness to new experiences. When individuals approach challenges with a sense of curiosity rather than fear, they are more likely to embrace opportunities for growth and learning. This willingness to learn and adapt fuels motivation and drives individuals to pursue their goals with persistence and resilience.

The practice of gratitude, often associated with mindfulness, can also enhance motivation. By focusing on the positive aspects of life and expressing gratitude for what one has, individuals can shift their mindset from scarcity to abundance. This positive outlook fosters a sense of contentment and satisfaction, which can be a powerful motivator. When individuals feel grateful for their current circumstances, they are more likely to be motivated to build on their successes and strive for further achievements.

Mindfulness can improve motivation by enhancing emotional regulation. When individuals are mindful, they are better able to manage their emotions and respond to situations with composure. This emotional balance is crucial for maintaining motivation, as it prevents individuals from becoming overwhelmed by setbacks or negative emotions. By staying calm and centered, individuals can navigate challenges with confidence and maintain their motivation even in the face of adversity.

Incorporating mindfulness into daily routines can create a supportive environment for motivation. Simple practices, such as setting aside time for meditation or mindful breathing, can help individuals cultivate a mindful mindset. Additionally, incorporating mindfulness into everyday activities, such as eating or walking, can reinforce the habit of being present and focused. By making mindfulness a regular part of life, individuals can create a foundation for sustained motivation and personal growth.

Mindfulness can enhance motivation by fostering a sense of connection and community. When individuals practice mindfulness, they often become more empathetic and compassionate towards others. This sense of connection can be a powerful motivator, as individuals are more likely to be inspired by the achievements and support of those around them. By cultivating meaningful relationships and a sense of belonging, individuals can draw motivation from their social networks and work towards common goals.

The journey of integrating mindfulness and motivation is unique to each individual, and it requires patience and commitment. It is not about achieving a state of constant motivation but rather developing the ability to harness mindfulness to sustain motivation over time. By embracing mindfulness, individuals can unlock their potential for personal and professional growth, experiencing life with greater purpose and fulfillment.